W9-ARE-173

First published in
the United States in 1990 by
Gloucester Press
387 Park Avenue South
New York NY 10016

Design: David West
Children's Book Design
Editor: Margaret Mulvihill
Picture Research: Cecilia Weston-Baker
Illustrator: Peter Harper

The author, Dr John Bradley, is the author of numerous books on World War II. He is an expert on Eastern Europe and international relations.

The consultant, Dr John Pimlott, teaches War Studies at the Royal Military Academy, Sandhurst, England. He is the author of many books on military history.

Printed in Belgium

Library of Congress Cataloging-in-Publication Data
Bradley, John (John S.N.)
Churchill / John Bradley.
p. cm. -- (World War II biographies)
Summary: Presents the life and accomplishments of Winston Churchill, focusing on his role as prime minister of the United Kingdom during World War II.
ISBN 0-531-17227-9
1. Churchill, Winston, Sir, 1874-1965 -- Juvenile literature. 2. Prime ministers -- Great Britain -- Biography -- Juvenile literature. 3. Great Britain -- Politics and government -- 20th century -- Juvenile literature. 4. World War, 1939-1945 -- Biography -- Juvenile literature. [1. Churchill, Winston, Sir, 1874-1965. 2. Prime ministers. 3. World War, 1939-1945.]
I. Title II. Series.
DA 566. 9. C5B66 1990
941. 082' 092 -- dc 20
[B]
[92] 89-81613 CIP AC

CONTENTS

WORLD WAR II BIOGRAPHIES

CHURCHILL AND THE BRITISH

JOHN BRADLEY

Winston Churchill was the man who led Britain throughout World War II. He has been described as Britain's savior and when the odds seemed firmly stacked against him, he persevered and led Britain through five hard years of fighting to the final victory against Nazi Germany. He took many controversial decisions, such as the bombing of Germany, for which he has been criticized. This book examines his prewar career and describes how he became Britain's prime minister and triumphed over Hitler.

GLOUCESTER PRESS
New York : London : Toronto : Sydney

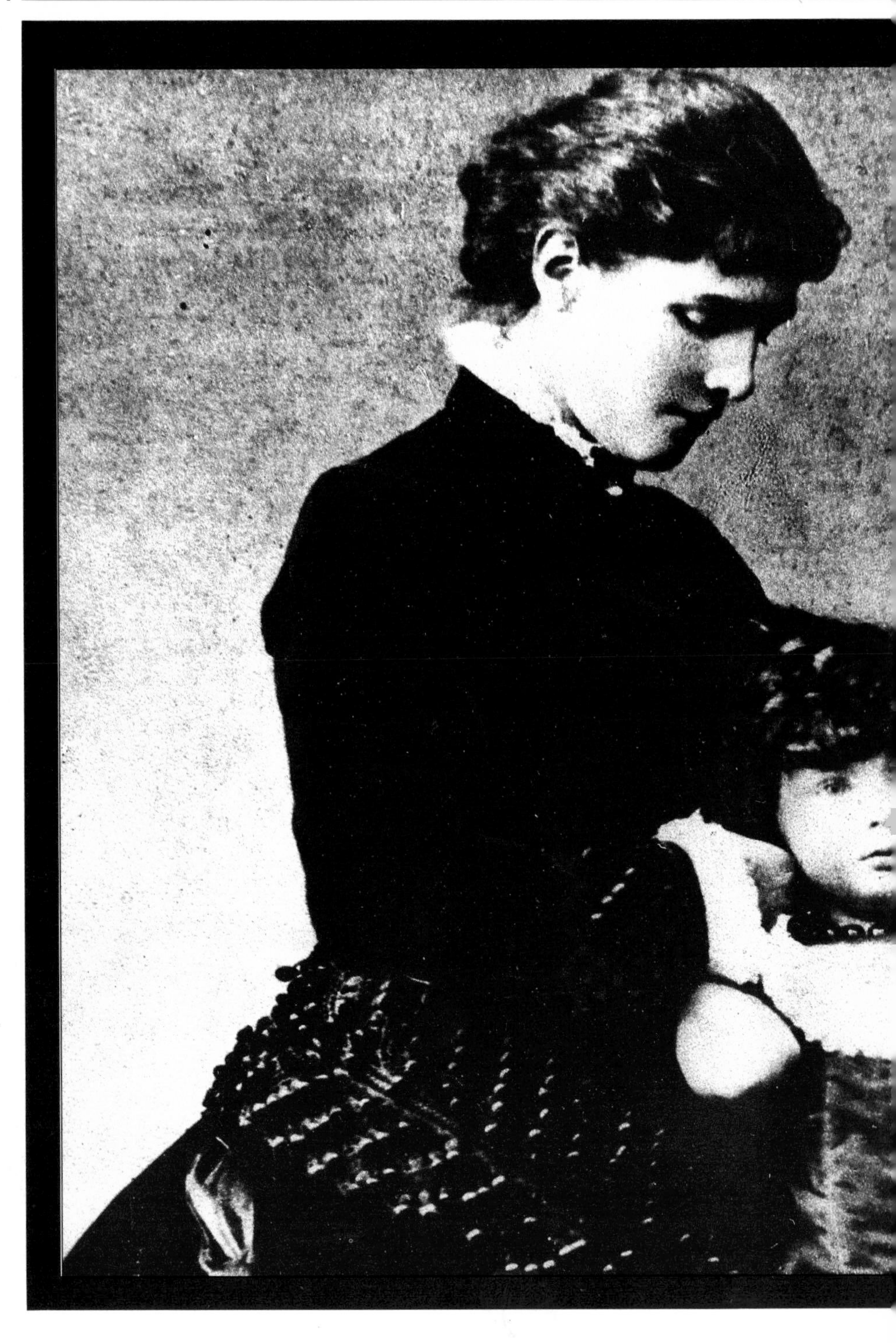

SOLDIER AND POLITICIAN

Winston Spencer Churchill was born, prematurely, at Blenheim Palace on November 30, 1874. As the eldest son of Lord Randolph Churchill and a grandson of the seventh Duke of Marlborough, this baby came into the world with a silver spoon in his mouth. Even so, no one, not even his fond parents, suspected that 91 years later, in 1965, Winston Churchill would be mourned throughout the world and celebrated for a lifetime of spectacular achievements.

Winston Churchill with his mother Jennie Jerome. She was only 20 when he was born. The Churchills had a long military tradition. The first Duke of Marlborough was a famous 17th and 18th century general, who led Britain's army to victories against the French.

Childhood

Churchill's mother was a beautiful and cultivated American woman. Even before her marriage to an English lord, 19 year-old Jennie Jerome was an aristocrat in all but title. She was thoroughly at home in high society and first met Lord Randolph at a ball aboard a yacht belonging to the heir to the imperial throne of Russia, which was moored off the Isle of Wight for the sailing season. After only a few days of waltzing and dining and talking, Lord Randolph proposed to her. Both of the couple's families objected to the speed of the romance, and so Lord Randolph agreed to stand for parliament before getting married. He was elected as a Member of Parliament (M.P.) in April 1874 and in that same month Jennie Jerome became Lady Randolph Churchill.

Winston Churchill's parents were extremely busy and public people. He had to adore his lively mother from a distance. To compensate for her absence from his early everyday life he had a devoted nanny, Mrs Everest. To her he poured out his early troubles and when she died, the 20 year-old Winston was at her bedside. As for his brilliant father, he was also distant. Lord Randolph Churchill's political career began in the year of Churchill's birth and very soon he was a prominent Conservative politician, seen by many as a future prime minister. Winston Churchill had a similar personality to his father. He was a great orator and he liked championing unpopular, or at least unfashionable, causes. Lord Randolph Churchill believed, for example, that to survive in the modern world, Conservatism had to appeal to the working

man, and he had the common touch. However, soon after he had been made Chancellor of the Exchequer, Lord Randolph Churchill disagreed with his Cabinet colleagues about military spending and resigned. After this, although he was only 40, his career as a major politician was over.

After two prep schools, the first of which was very miserable and brutal, Churchill went to Harrow School. Here he was a reasonably all-round pupil and his father urged him in the direction of a career in the army. After his third attempt at the entrance examination, Churchill was admitted to Sandhurst to be trained as an officer. He thoroughly enjoyed his training, and his sympathy with army life was to be important in

The young Winston at Harrow School. He was a keen fencer and won a Public School competition. Although he did not enjoy Latin and Greek, he was good at other subjects and developed a clear style in essay writing.

his future career as the political leader of a nation at war – Britain during World War II.

In due course Churchill was commissioned as an officer in the Fourth Hussars and it seemed that he was on a smooth course to a successful career in the upper echelons of the army. However, during his time at Sandhurst Churchill had grown closer to his father and he had begun to nurse political ambitions. Lord Randolph Churchill's sudden death at the age of 45 was a terrible blow: "All my dreams of comradeship with him, of entering parliament at his side and in his support, were ended. There remained for me only to pursue his aims and vindicate his memory." In some consolation, he did begin to enjoy a closer relationship with Jennie Churchill, who was more like an elder sister to him than a mother.

The dashing war correspondent

The young Churchill wanted to write as well as

Churchill (right) as a prisoner of war in South Africa, 1899. He was captured after the Boers derailed the train he was traveling on. Churchill organized a spirited fight to resist being taken prisoner. He managed to escape from the camp and after crossing Boer country was welcomed back in British territory as a hero.

fight. To further this desire, he went on a personal rather than official initiative, to war-torn Cuba in 1895. The result was a series of vivid newspaper articles by a journalist who understood military strategies and was not afraid of getting in the line of fire. Although he soon rejoined his cavalry regiment in India, it was plain that Churchill was a restless and understretched officer. He had to be more than a soldier. Even more than the actual campaigning, he loved to observe, report, describe and evaluate his experiences. Throughout his stay in India he continued to read widely and in 1898 he published his first observation, *The Story of the Malakand Field Force*. This was the campaign in the northwestern frontier of India in which he took part. In the same year, he got himself posted to the Sudan, took part in the battle of Omdurman, and wrote *The River War*.

In 1899 Churchill went to South Africa to describe the war between Britain and the Boers, but on this occasion he was a highly paid war correspondent rather than a soldier who did journalism on the side. Captured and imprisoned by the Boers, Churchill managed to escape. He succeeded in reaching a British base after a series of hair-raising adventures. When he was on the run a reward was offered for his capture, dead or alive. His account of how he fled from a well-guarded prison to be concealed among sacks of coal on a supply train, and jumped to eventual safety from that train made him instantly famous. He became known as the man who had escaped the Boers. He spent a year in South Africa and rejoined the army. Then Winston Churchill stood

in 1900 as a Conservative member of Parliament for Oldham and was elected with a small majority.

The young politician

Rather typically, Churchill did not immediately settle down to the life of a member of Parliament. To earn extra income he went on a lecture tour of the United States, returning to make his first speech in the House of Commons in February 1901. Over the next 50 years Churchill was to make nearly 2,000 expertly planned speeches. Although he did not always persuade his audiences of his point of view, he could always impress them and he was never dull. For the next three years, he concentrated on joining the political opposition to Joseph Chamberlain's attempt to introduce trade barriers. Like his father, he was not afraid of being unpopular, even with his own party. Increasingly, he found the Conservatives dull in the face of social and economic inequalities. When his relatively radical opinions made his position with the Conservatives of the day impossible, he joined the Liberals in 1904.

Churchill, not for the first time, saw himself as putting country before party. His association with the Liberal party, which was unusual for a military man with his family background, was to last for 20 years. It resulted in immediate political promotion and December 1905 saw Winston Churchill installed as Under-Secretary of State for the Colonies. At this time his biography of Lord Randolph Churchill was published, and in his defense of his father's maverick reputation, he was to some extent defending his own very individual career

A photograph of Churchill taken at the time of his election to parliament in 1900. He had stood for Oldham in 1899, but failed to be elected. After his exploits in South Africa, he was a popular hero and was elected at the age of 26.

against people who said he was a traitor to his first political party, the Conservatives.

In 1908 the Liberal Churchill's star was still rising and he joined Herbert Henry Asquith's government as president of the Board of Trade. In that same year he married Clementine Hozier and, in his own words, "lived happily ever afterward." They had four daughters, one of whom died as a child, and one son. Throughout his stormy political career Churchill enjoyed a stable and happy home life. Clementine Churchill frequently accompanied him on his political campaigns.

Churchill and World War I

After his stint at the Board of Trade, Churchill became Home Secretary. These were the years (1910-11) of the "Labor Unrest" and Churchill would be remembered by many working people and by the women who were campaigning for the vote as the man in charge of the repression of strikes and protests. Many people who later respected Churchill's instincts with regard to foreign policy were less inclined to trust him on home affairs when they remembered his days as Home Secretary. This was to be one of the factors explaining his electoral defeat after World War II.

However, his next appointment in September 1911 was as First Lord of the Admiralty, a position dear to his personal interests. He immediately made himself an expert on all aspects of naval warfare and this responsibility lasted until 1915, a year after the outbreak of World War I. But in that year there was widespread criticism of his war actions, particularly the disastrous troop landings at Gallipoli in the eastern Mediterranean.

In response to such criticism, he resigned. It was at this stage in his life, when his career seemed shattered, that he became an enthusiastic amateur artist. However, it was not like Churchill to retire to his easel and his books. In November 1915 he went to war as a soldier, spending six months on active duty as an officer in the trenches on the Western Front in France.

In 1916 he tried to get back into politics. After all, he was only 42 and a politician of considerable experience. In 1917, in spite of resignation threats from the Conservatives in his coalition government, prime minister David Lloyd George insisted on making Churchill Minister of Munitions. By 1919, after the end of World War I,

Winston Churchill with David Lloyd George. In 1915, after British Empire troops failed to establish themselves in Gallipoli and many of them had died, Churchill left active politics for the army. After six months' experience of battle, Churchill wanted to get back into politics, but Conservative politicians were set against this. Eventually Lloyd George got his way and Churchill became Minister of Munitions.

Churchill was Secretary of State for War and became involved with the demobilization of the armies, with the intervention against the revolution in Russia and with the struggle against the independence movement in Ireland. He then spent another year as Secretary of State for the Colonies.

With the defeat of the Liberal coalition government in a general election, Churchill was again in a difficult situation. He had been defeated as a parliamentary candidate in 1922 and he failed when he tried to stand again as an anti-socialist candidate. When the Labor government of 1924 recognized Bolshevik Russia he was furious. Even without a seat in the Commons, he campaigned on public platforms and through a ceaseless flow of newspaper articles. In 1924 he decided to join the Conservative party again, returning to parliament as M.P. for Epping and a place as Chancellor of the Exchequer in Stanley Baldwin's government.

Churchill's position with this administration was uncomfortable. He took a very uncompromising line against the miners in the General Strike of 1926 and he was opposed to any return to the Gold Standard. However, many Conservatives regarded Churchill as relatively liberal. Many of his new colleagues disliked his budgets, which tried to lessen the tax burden on small incomes. Asquith described Churchill as "a Chimborazo or Everest among the sandhills of the Baldwin Cabinet."

The years of isolation

For the ten years, from the fall of the Conservative government in 1929 to the outbreak of World War

II, Churchill was in parliament without any ministerial responsibility. Already he was seen as part of history, an old man, now in his sixties, who was not relevant to the future: "Here I am, discarded, cast away, marooned, rejected and disliked." But if he thought strongly enough about something, he didn't mind being isolated and unpopular. Increasingly, the state of Germany was a focus for his enormous energies.

Churchill had been concerned that the Treaty of Versailles, which formally ended World War I, held the seeds of another world war because it was too severe toward Germany. In 1933 he was alarmed by the rise of Adolf Hitler, who was now openly seeking to reverse that settlement and rearm Germany. But this fierce and vigilant attitude of Churchill's was considered old-fashioned and cantankerous. It did not help that his potential allies were the very socialists and communists against whom he had campaigned so vehemently in the past. Even though he was honestly opposed to war for its own sake, it was easy to attack Churchill as a warmonger. He was going too far. He took the threat posed to Europe by Hitler so seriously that he even proposed an alliance between Britain, France and Russia. But Churchill's warnings and his suggestions were ignored. When he spoke in the House of Commons some fellow M.P.s walked out, while others mocked him.

Undaunted, Churchill continued to make his speeches. He also made contact with individual politicians who, even if they differed over matters of domestic policy, were at one with him in their opposition to the government's appeasement of

Hitler. In March 1938, when Hitler annexed Austria, Churchill called upon the government to rearm the country and to prepare for war: "If our defenses are weak, we must seek allies, if we seek allies, alliances involve commitments."

Later that year Hitler demanded a large area of Czechoslovakia, and Churchill condemned the Munich Agreement, by which prime minister Neville Chamberlain gave in to this outrageous move. By then, the urgency of the threat from Hitler, and Britain's weak position in the face of it, was crystal clear. Churchill was vindicated and popular opinion was in favor of a government job for the prophet in the wilderness.

Neville Chamberlain did not want Churchill in his government. Churchill continued to criticize Chamberlain's foreign policy, but to no avail. Then, in September 1939, only two weeks after Germany and the Soviet Union had signed a secret war pact, Hitler invaded Poland. Neville Chamberlain, who had pledged to defend Poland, now had to declare war on Germany. The situation Churchill had fought so hard to avoid had happened. If Churchill had been heeded, Britain might have been strong enough to deter Hitler, and there might have been a defensive alliance between Britain, France and the Soviet Union instead of the Nazi-Soviet Pact.

Churchill arrives at the Admiralty on September 4, 1939. When news of his appointment broke, a message was sent to Britain's navy "Winston is back."

Still, it was perhaps not too late to learn from the mistakes of the 1930s. On the same day as the declaration of war Churchill was appointed First Lord of the Admiralty, the very post he had held in 1914. After ten years in the wilderness, Churchill was again in office at the age of 65.

The King to his People

CHURCHILL AS PRIME MINISTER

After so many years of appeasement Hitler did not take Britain's declaration of war too seriously. Knowing Neville Chamberlain's instincts, he was certain that peace would be reestablished between Germany and Britain after the successful *Blitzkrieg*, or "lightning war," in Poland. Hitler's deputy, Hermann Göring, was much less optimistic when he heard of Churchill's appointment, and he was right.

Churchill leaves the prime minister's residence to address the House of Commons with the grim news that France has been defeated, June 1940. This was a dark hour for Britain, which was now alone in the fight against Germany.

The public, the politicians and the armed forces took Churchill's appointment to mean that this time Britain meant business. On the day after his appointment, at the war cabinet meeting, he suggested immediate steps to relieve the Polish front, most importantly a joint bombardment by Anglo-French air forces of the German fortifications, known as the Siegfried Line. By then he knew of the sinking, by German U-boats (submarines), of the steamship *Athenia* off Ireland, in which American passengers had drowned with British ones. Although he urged his colleagues to take up this matter with the United States government, his position was still so individual that he was even accused of having personally placed a bomb on the *Athenia* in an effort to rouse American opinion against Hitler. Churchill also ordered convoy sailing for British ships, whereby groups of merchant ships sailed together protected by warships, in all the oceans. He fired so many instructions around the Admiralty that his memos became known as "First Lord's Prayers."

Churchill, who was a member of the new Land Forces Committee as well as First Lord of the Admiralty, was phenomenally active as a military strategist, a politician, a diplomat and a general morale-raiser. He did not give in to the temptation to say "I told you so." Instead, he put a finger into every fighting pie. He insisted that Britain could only win the fight against Germany in close co-operation with its allies, particularly with France, but also, hopefully, with the United States. It was also of the utmost importance that the whole of the country's economy, not just the armed forces, was geared up to fight the war against Hitler.

Churchill's initial success in getting the British Expeditionary Force to France without mishap added to his growing prestige. But some of his government colleagues were still alarmed by his other plans. He wanted to open up the Balkan front, get Belgium involved in the war, ensure a British presence in the Baltic Sea, and gain the neutralization of Norway, Sweden and Denmark. In these plans he did have public support, in spite of several initial disasters and a generally darkening situation. But as the war widened, British interests were threatened in the Balkans and because of indecision, Denmark and Norway were occupied by the German army. When Churchill's plan to send troops to Norway was approved by the government, it was too late. The Germans got there before Britain and Churchill had to declare: "We have been completely outwitted."

German troops during the invasion of Norway. Churchill wanted a special naval force to be sent to Norway to forestall a German invasion. By the time the naval force left Britain on April 5 it was too late. The German invasion started on April 9 and the British and French did not land in Norway until April 16.

Churchill's real moment of complete authority came at the same time as another catastrophe, this time in France. The British and French allies had been certain of Hitler's intention to invade France. They captured, or otherwise obtained, the German invasion plans, which forced Hitler to change them and postpone the invasion many times. The Allies had agreed with Belgium that in the event of that country being invaded they could move their armies into that area. But this was a strategic error because Hitler planned to invade France through the Ardennes. On May 10, 1940, the German armies simultaneously invaded the Netherlands and Belgium in the north, drawing Anglo-French troops forward into Belgium. On May 13, having infiltrated the "impassable" Ardennes, German *Panzers* (tanks) crossed the Meuse at Sedan and

Churchill (left), Clement Attlee (center left), Clementine Churchill (center right) and Anthony Eden (right) in August 1941. Attlee joined Churchill's coaltion government as deputy prime minister. Eden was close to Churchill and served as his foreign minister for most of the war.

headed for the Channel coast, cutting off the Allied forces in Belgium.

While this was beginning to unfold the British parliament was debating the disastrous Norwegian expedition. More than one hundred Conservative M.P.s voted against Neville Chamberlain or abstained. Chamberlain, who was terminally ill with cancer, resigned and Winston Churchill was the only leader of a wartime all-party government who was acceptable to Liberal and Labor M.P.s. So it was that on May 10, 1940, Winston Churchill became the undisputed political leader of a Britain at war. When he went to bed that night he felt "conscious of a profound sense of relief. At last I had authority to give directions over a whole scene. I felt as if I were walking with Destiny, and that all my past life had been but a preparation for this hour and this trial...."

With his speeches Churchill created an atmosphere in which people felt able to win, by sheer obstinacy if necessary. He was generous in his praise of those who had shown courage, and always, even in the face of appalling odds, humorous and optimistic. By contrast, Neville Chamberlain had seemed dismally defeatist. Even people who had reason to mistrust Winston Churchill in the past now began to have affection for his personality. His eccentric clothes, his cigars, his familiar voice, his "V" for victory gestures and his enthusiasm for every effort made him the right man to hold the country together. Upon his appointment as prime minister, Churchill shouldered the blame for the failure in Norway, but typically he went on to speak of ultimate victory: "I have nothing to offer but blood, toil, tears and sweat." His coalition government was a broad one, with Clement Attlee, leader of the Labor party, as his deputy, and Lord Halifax, a Conservative, as the Foreign Secretary. Outsiders were also recruited, including Lord

DEFEAT IN FRANCE

Churchill became prime minister as the British and French armies faced defeat in France. The German *Panzer* armies swept through the Ardennes and were able to encircle British and French troops in northern France. Hitler was afraid that the infantry was too far behind the tanks so he ordered a 48-hour delay. This gave the British the opportunity to organize the evacuation of troops from Dunkirk. French troops were demoralized and short of equipment. They tried to defend the capital, Paris, but the Germans took the city on June 14.

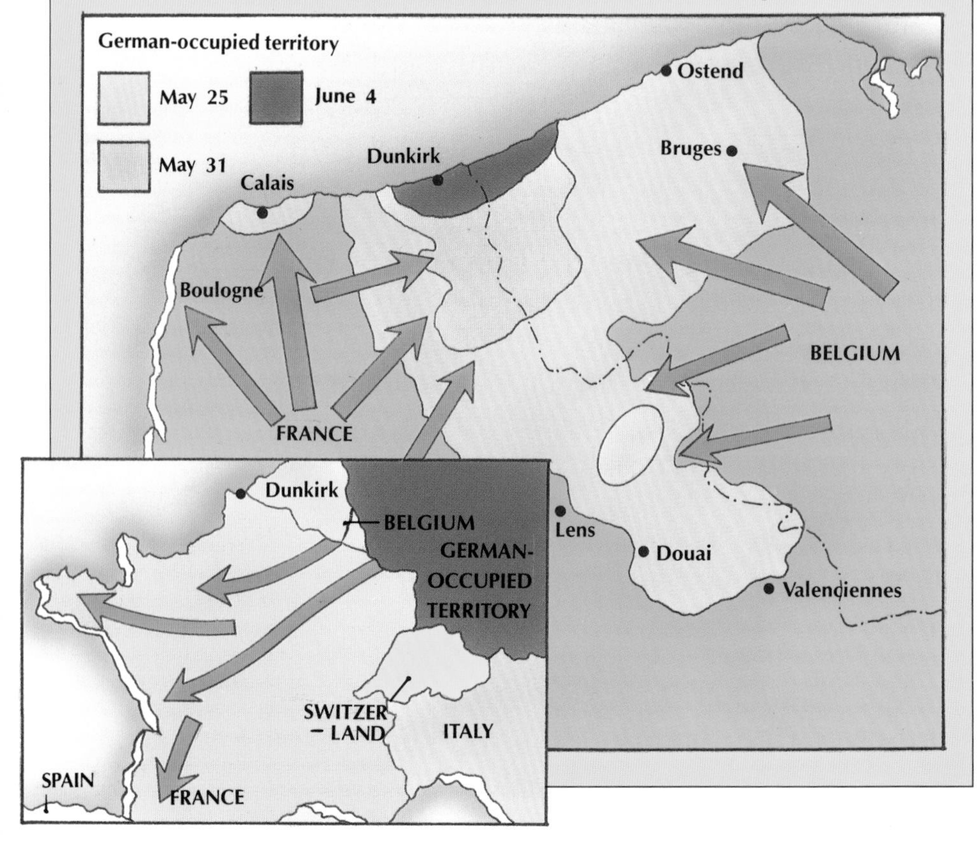

Beaverbrook, the newspaper owner, and Ernest Bevin, the trade unionist. This emergency government was now given virtual dictatorial powers over the life and property of the British people. But was it too late?

By the end of May German armies had reached the northern French coast. Belgium and Holland had surrendered and the British Expeditionary Force was encircled on the beaches at Dunkirk. Over a period of eight days British, Dutch, French and Belgian ships of all sizes carried over 338,000 men back to English shores. It was a heroic feat. The British Expeditionary Forces had been saved.

Churchill tried desperately to keep France in the war and at considerable risk to his own safety, he went as late as June 13 to Tours to meet with French leaders. Three days later he offered the French a Franco-British Union with common citizenship. However, the French government resigned and the new one, led by Marshal Henri Philippe Pétain, sued for an armistice with the German invaders. Only General Charles de Gaulle wanted to continue the struggle and he was encouraged in his efforts to organize a French resistance movement. In the meantime, the Soviet Union's Red Army invaded the Baltic republics, and so Josef Stalin of the Soviet Union and Hitler appeared to have divided continental Europe between them.

In the middle of these misfortunes Churchill exhorted his people to go on fighting, if need be alone. "Let us brace ourselves to our duty and so bear ourselves that if the British Commonwealth and Empire lasts a thousand years men will still say: 'This was their finest hour.'"

THE WARTIME LEADER

Even when the German advance seemed unstoppable, Churchill never wavered in his belief that Britain could and would win. In June 1940, when the last soldiers were being rescued from Dunkirk, he rallied the country with one of his most famous speeches: "We shall fight on the beaches, we shall fight on the landing grounds, we shall fight in the fields and in the streets, we shall fight in the hills; we shall never surrender."

British and French soldiers line up, waiting to be evacuated from Dunkirk, June 1940. From May 26 to June 4 all kinds of craft, from destroyers to private motor cruisers, brought the men to England.

In July 1940 British shipping in the Channel came under heavy attack from the Germans. It became apparent that the Germans were concentrating some 250 ships and 100,000 men for an invasion of Britain, "Operation Sealion." Churchill replied with the announcement of a worldwide blockade of Germany and this almost immediately brought about conflict with Pétain's regime in France, which was known as the Vichy government. As a result, French ships in British-controlled harbors were requisitioned and those at Mers-el-Kebir,

A German bomber shot down somewhere in Scotland, 1939. It was the first enemy aircraft to be shot down over Britain and a taste of things to come.

Algeria were sunk with a loss of about 1,300 lives.

The Channel Islands were occupied by the Germans, but their air offensive against the Royal Air Force (RAF) was not so successful. Though numerically inferior, the RAF made use of a new invention, radar, and managed to resist successfully the German onslaught on its airfields.

On August 24 the Germans mistakenly attacked London. In retaliation Churchill ordered a raid on Berlin on August 25 and 26, which was carried out without causing very much material damage.

British fighter pilots scramble to get to their planes, 1940. It was the bravery of the fighter crews that won the Battle of Britain.

THE BATTLE OF BRITAIN

Hitler ordered the air attack on Britain to start on July 10, 1940. The German *Luftwaffe* had 2,200 aircraft against the RAF's 591 fighters. However, the RAF had the advantage of an early warning system, known as radar. At first the Germans attacked the Channel ports and shipping, but after a month started bombing RAF airfields. This nearly worked as RAF losses mounted, but then the Germans switched to bombing London and other cities on September 7, known as the "Blitz." The Battle of Britain reached a peak on September 15. By this time German losses were so high that two days later Hitler postponed the proposed invasion of Britain. German nighttime raids on British cities continued until May 1941. During the battle the Hawker Hurricane proved it could easily outfly the Messerschmitt Bf 109, and Junkers Ju 87 divebombers suffered very high losses.

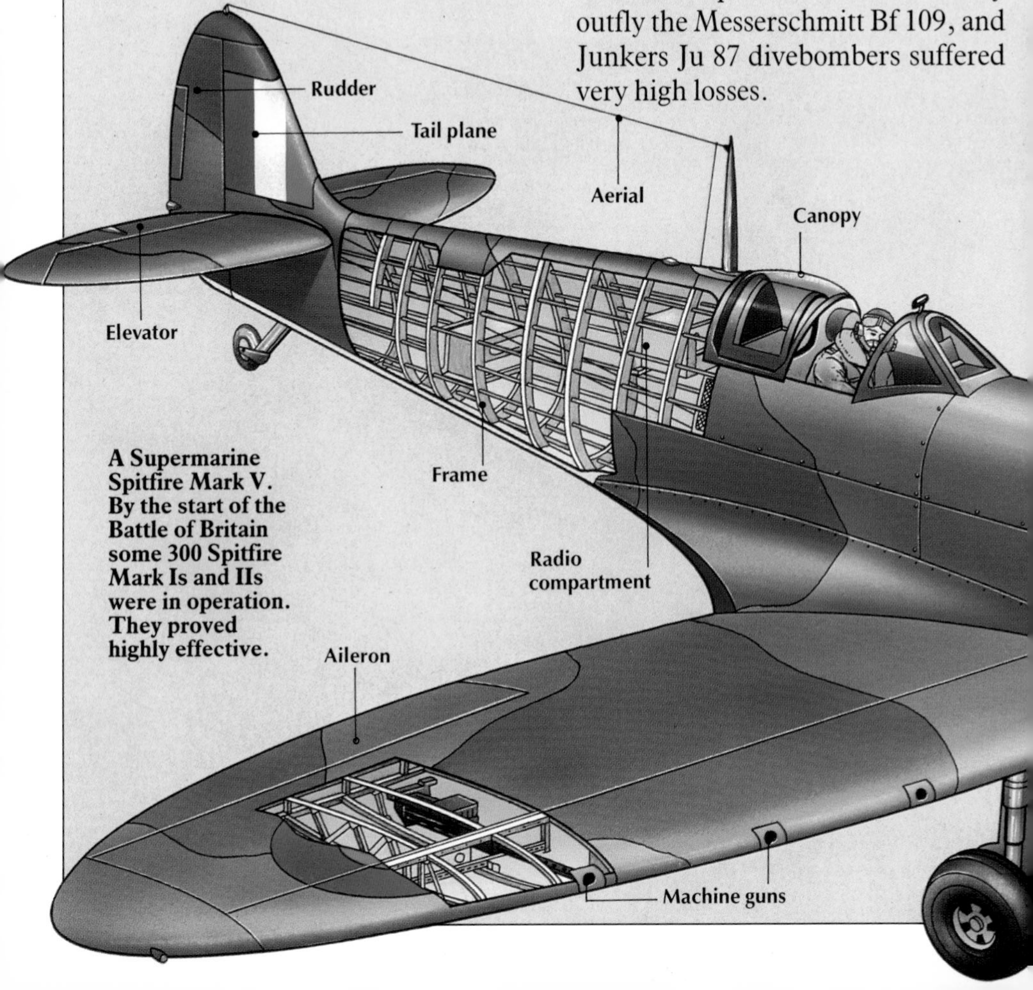

A Supermarine Spitfire Mark V. By the start of the Battle of Britain some 300 Spitfire Mark Is and IIs were in operation. They proved highly effective.

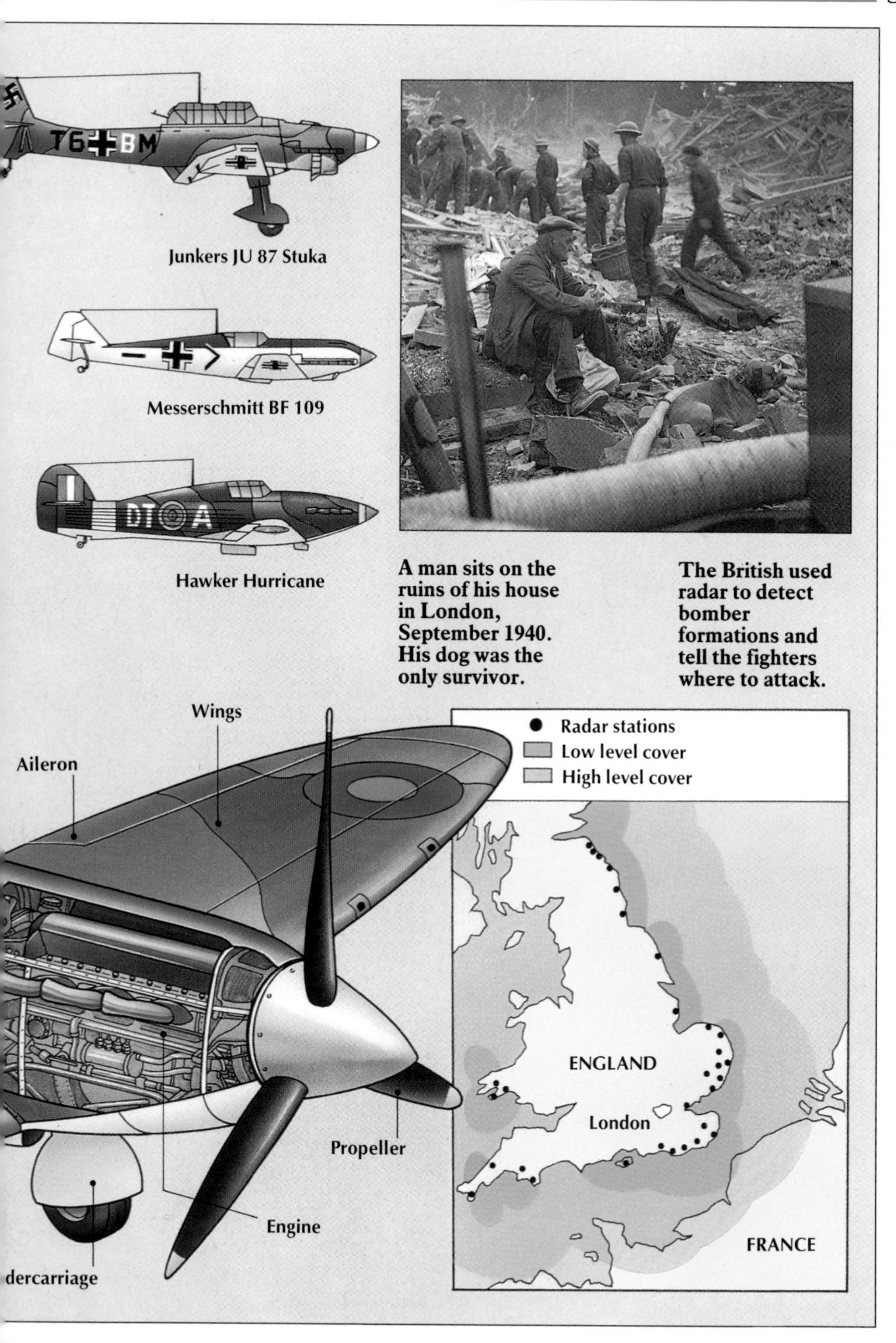

A man sits on the ruins of his house in London, September 1940. His dog was the only survivor.

The British used radar to detect bomber formations and tell the fighters where to attack.

Its psychological value as a morale-raiser was enormous. In September the *Luftwaffe* started to attack British cities and the Battle of Britain raged for the next months, but still the Germans failed to destroy the RAF. Hitler had to postpone the planned invasion of Britain. Paying tribute to the RAF pilots in parliament, Churchill said: "Never in the field of human conflict was so much owed by so many to so few."

From the fall of France in June 1940 until Hitler's invasion of the Soviet Union a year later, Britain stood alone in the struggle against Germany in Europe. As Germany's ally and one of the Axis powers, Benito Mussolini's Italy began to attack British possessions in the Mediterranean and in Africa. At this point Japan joined the German-Italian alliance and this brought the United States back into the picture. Threatened by the rise of the Japanese in the East, the United States gave new support to Britain. In exchange for bases in Newfoundland and the West Indies, the Americans agreed to supply Britain with 50 outdated destroyers. In spite of his friendly relations with Churchill, President Franklin D. Roosevelt was not yet in a strong enough political position to offer an outright alliance.

The RAF intensified its bombing of German cities during 1941, after it had failed to achieve much damage when attacking Germany's oil supplies. However, the Battle of the Atlantic was not going well, as German U-boats were sinking many of the merchant ships bringing supplies to Britain, whose food prospects looked increasingly grim. While the German alliance was swelled by

Hungary and Slovakia (Vichy France was officially neutral), Francisco Franco of Spain, a natural ally of fascism, decided to remain neutral.

The first victories in the field brought encouragement. The invading Italian forces in Egypt were destroyed and 130,000 Italians became prisoners of war. In turn Libya was invaded and Australian troops proved particularly successful in taking Bardia and Tobruk. Then British forces scored two more successes in Eritrea and Somaliland. Hitler managed to reverse the situation in Libya, however, by sending General Erwin Rommel and his Afrika Korps to North Africa.

In March 1941 Hitler became active in the Balkans, upsetting practically all of Churchill's plans in that region. Bulgaria joined the Axis powers and in April Hitler came to Italy's assistance and attacked Greece. After some hesitation, Yugoslavia was destroyed and occupied by the Germans. In that part of the world only Turkey remained neutral.

When Germany threatened increased U-boat activity in the Atlantic and heavier bombing of Britain, the United States reacted by occupying Greenland and moving closer to an outright alliance with Britain. The Lend Lease Agreement, whereby Britain would get military equipment free and pay for it after the war, was signed. In all of these negotiations Churchill was the individual who represented Britain's struggle, both the victories and the defeats. Once the danger of a German invasion had been removed, his personal style of leadership was subject to what were by now familiar criticisms. His personal courage was in no doubt –

he had, for example, refused to evacuate the government from London – but perhaps he was too old and there were too many people around him whose only virtue was the fact that they agreed with him all of the time. To keep such critics at bay Churchill desperately needed to tilt the world balance of power in Britain's favor. But before there could be victories there had to be defeats.

One defeat that led to ultimate victory was Hitler's sudden invasion of the Soviet Union in June 1941. Within months the Germans were within sight of Moscow, Leningrad was besieged and Kharkov was occupied. Only the dread Russian winter halted the advance of the German forces. But now the Soviet Union was Britain's ally, Churchill pledging Stalin as much aid as Britain could manage. August 1941 saw one result of this new alliance: joint Soviet and British forces intervened in Iran to forestall Hitler's agents there.

In August 1941 Churchill and Roosevelt met in Newfoundland and signed the Atlantic Charter. This was a joint declaration of peace aims and included the principles of no-territorial gains and self-government for all nations. The Japanese attack on the American Pacific fleet at Pearl Harbor on December 7 shocked the United States and enabled Roosevelt to enter the war against Germany in the West and Japan in the East. The Japanese armies now launched a series of lightning attacks against British, French and Dutch colonies. When the British colony of Malaysia and Singapore was captured by the Japanese, in February 1942, Churchill had to respond to his critics at home by changing some of his ministers. But with the United

States and the Soviet Union now in the war with Britain he could speak of ultimate victory with more confidence than ever before. Against security and health advice he insisted on going in person to the United States. While he was on the battleship taking him across the Atlantic he was informed of the success of Soviet counterattacks around Moscow. He immediately telegraphed Stalin to tell him of his relief: "I have never felt so sure of the outcome of the war." Once in Washington, he persuaded the American president and Congress to establish a joint War Council and a joint committee of all the Chiefs of Staff for winning the war. There were, he thought, "three phases" of the war to come: closing the ring; liberating the populations; final assault on the German citadel.

The year 1942 opened with a declaration of the United Nations' opposition to the Axis powers, signed by 26 countries. It endorsed the Atlantic Charter and gave Churchill an important international vote of confidence in his conduct of the war. However, this political triumph could not mask a desperate military situation. In the Far East, the Philippines fell and Japanese troops landed on the Solomon Islands and New Guinea. In May 1942 the Afrika Korps pushed the Eighth Army out of Libya, threatening Egypt. In the Soviet Union the German armies resumed their offensive in the southern sector, forestalling Stalin's counter offensive at Kharkov and breaking through toward the Volga and the Caspian Sea in the south.

In June 1942, faced with these setbacks Churchill decided to visit Washington again. This visit was, in a way, Churchill's "finest hour." Partly because of his American mother and partly because of the many transatlantic friendships and contacts he had built up in his career, Churchill felt very at home among the American leaders. With great skill he persuaded Roosevelt to accept his views on future strategy. After the battle of the Coral Sea and of Midway in May-June 1942, which checked the Japanese advance in the Pacific Ocean, Roosevelt agreed that the bulk of the United States' immense resources would go to the European theater of war. This was known as "Germany First." The Western Allies were going to drive the Germans from North Africa and Occupied Europe, even if it meant opening up second, third or fourth fronts. With Churchill's approval, Major-General Dwight Eisenhower was appointed US commander,

President Franklin Roosevelt (left) and General Dwight Eisenhower on their way to the Cairo Conference in November 1943. Churchill and Roosevelt met throughout the war to discuss Allied strategy and war aims.

European Theater, and in spite of recent losses in Libya and Egypt, a landing in Europe was to be planned.

There were some differences between the major Allies – Britain, the United States and the Soviet Union – about priorities. With his armies in retreat Stalin was at first reluctant to agree to the concentration on the Mediterranean Front. Roosevelt and Stalin were pressing for a second front to be opened up in France, and as soon as possible. Churchill did not think this was feasible yet. As if to prove his point, in July only 11 out of 35 merchant ships of a British PQ-17 convoy to Russia reached Archangel. A month later an Anglo-Canadian raid on the port of Dieppe was a disaster. Churchill worked as hard as ever, reorganizing the forces in Africa, even though he had suffered a heart attack. Because any announcement of the war leader's ill health would have been disastrous for morale, at his own request, Churchill's *angina pectoris* remained a secret until after his death.

British troops capture a German tank crew at El Alamein, November 1942.

With these new strategies in action, the second half of 1942 was a turning point. At El Alamein Britain's General Bernard Montgomery triumphed over Rommel, signaling the beginning of the end of the German presence in North Africa. To celebrate this first substantial victory in the field, church bells rang out all over Britain. Within a few days

THE NORTH AFRICA CAMPAIGN

Fighting in North Africa was very mobile. Rommel's Afrika Korps swept along the Libyan and Egyptian coast until they nearly reached Cairo during 1942. In November 1942 Montgomery finally threw the Germans back at El Alamein. On November 8 three Allied task forces landed in North Africa. By the end of the month Anglo-American forces were ready to move on to Tunisia. In December Axis reinforcements arrived, but by mid-May all Axis troops in North Africa had surrendered.

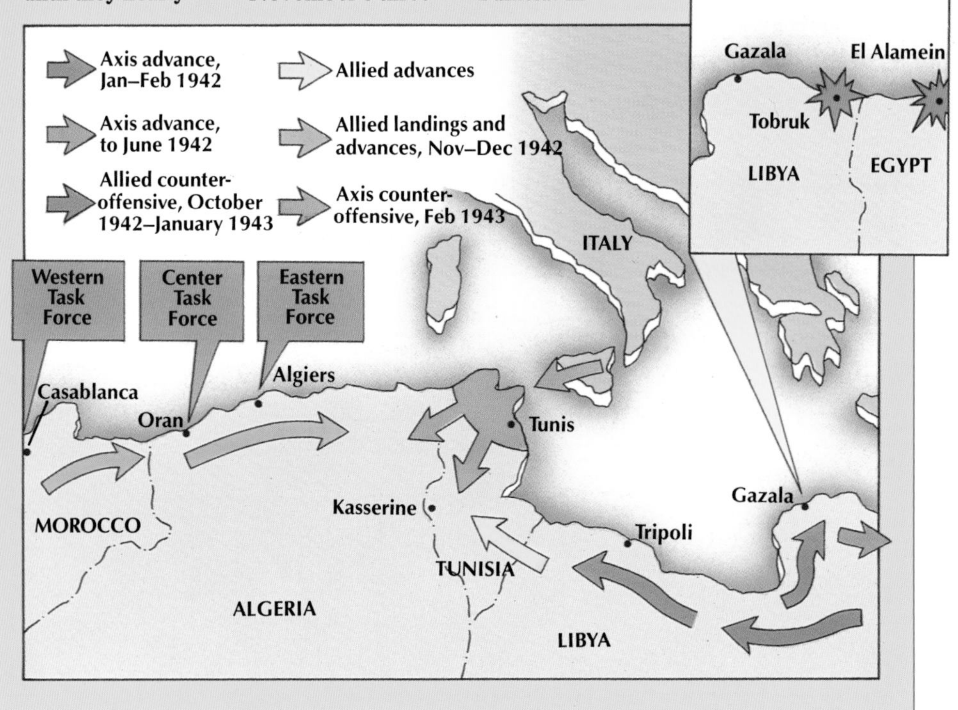

American and British troops had landed in Morocco and Algeria, confirming that triumph. Even though the Germans occupied the whole of France, the French fleet was scuttled in Toulon, so that there was no reinforcement of German naval forces. Moreover the Soviet armies finally stopped the German advance on the Volga, at Stalingrad. In Burma in late 1942 the British also stopped the Japanese advance. The tide was turning.

By February 1943 Field Marshal Friedrich Paulus and his Sixth Army had surrendered to the Russians at Stalingrad; the Allies advanced from Algiers and Egypt, Tripoli and Tunisia fell in May 1943; in August the Japanese army abandoned the Solomon Islands and began their long retreat; the RAF began to pound German cities and instead of hunting in the Atlantic, German U-boats were themselves being hunted. Churchill met Roosevelt three times during this momentous year. At Casablanca in January they decided that Italy should be the next target. They discussed the idea that the Axis powers should be told to surrender unconditionally. At Quebec a meeting with Stalin was arranged. Churchill was increasingly wary knowing that the Soviet leader would erode his influence with the American president. Later on that year Churchill and Roosevelt met with Stalin at Teheran.

More immediately, the war continued according to Churchill's grand design. The Allies landed successfully in Sicily and then on the Italian mainland. Mussolini was deposed and Italy formally surrendered. However, despite the fall of the Italian army, the German armies continued to struggle in that region and the battle over the Winter Line delayed the Allies' Italian advance for months. A combined American and British bombing raid on Hamburg in July 1943 did severe damage, while on the Eastern Front the Germans were falling back from Kharkov. Taganrog, the Donbass basin, Novorossiisk, Kremenchug and Smolensk were retaken by the Soviets. Churchill's influence over the Allies was waning. In the partnership with the United States, Britain was the junior power.

Churchill's fears about Britain's influence on the course of events were borne out at the Teheran summit meeting of November 1943. On the way there, Churchill met with Roosevelt and the Chinese leader, Chiang Kai-shek, and made a few decisions on the Far East, but there were no prior consultations for the summit. Roosevelt dealt directly with Stalin and when Roosevelt teased Churchill, describing him as a dictator, there was a gleam in the Soviet dictator's eyes.

Although he would do his utmost to strengthen the alliance with the Soviet Union so as to win the war, Churchill saw himself as dealing with a communist ogre. As for the Soviet leader, he was collaborating with a man he thought of as an arch-imperialist and reactionary. At this meeting Stalin wanted, and he got, a promise of an Allied landing in France as soon as possible, rather than a Balkan landing, which is what Churchill wanted. Churchill wanted to make sure the Soviets did not have too much influence there. Also, on Stalin's insistence, Germany would pay for the war with heavy reparations and territorial "adjustments," and this ran counter to Churchill's ideas. He had once described Hitler as "this monstrous product of former wrongs and shame," and he was concerned that yet another world war should not arise from the ashes of an unduly punishing postwar settlement.

Finally, Roosevelt's "unconditional surrender" became the official Allied aim. This meant that the Allies would not negotiate about an end to the war. Although Churchill now knew that the world and Britain's place among the superpowers was changing, he was able to telegraph to Clement Attlee: "We have had a grand day here, and relations between Britain, United States and USSR have never been so cordial and intimate. All war plans are agreed and concerted."

Stalin, Roosevelt and Churchill meet at the Teheran Conference in November 1943. They were known as the Big Three. This was the first occasion on which the three leaders met.

THE BATTLE OF THE ATLANTIC

This battle was waged between the German U-boats, fleet and aircraft and the merchant shipping and navies of the Allies. After the Fall of France, German U-boats were able to move along the Atlantic coast and attack Allied shipping. The Germans wanted to disrupt supplies coming from overseas to Britain and starve it into submission.

From early on the British organized convoys so that warships escorted groups of merchant ships. When the United States entered the war in December 1941 they did not immediately use the convoy syste
and Allied losses were high.

In April-May 1943 the Alli
inflicted heavy losses on the U-boa
in a series of convoy battles. Th
U-boats were withdrawn from th
Battle of the Atlantic. However, on
the Germans had worked out ne
tactics and got new weapons th
battle was on again until the end
the war.

Between 1939 and 1945, 785 U
boats were sunk and 28,000 Germa
sailors died. The Allies lost abo
2,800 merchant ships.

A British destroyer under attack from U-boat torpedoes.

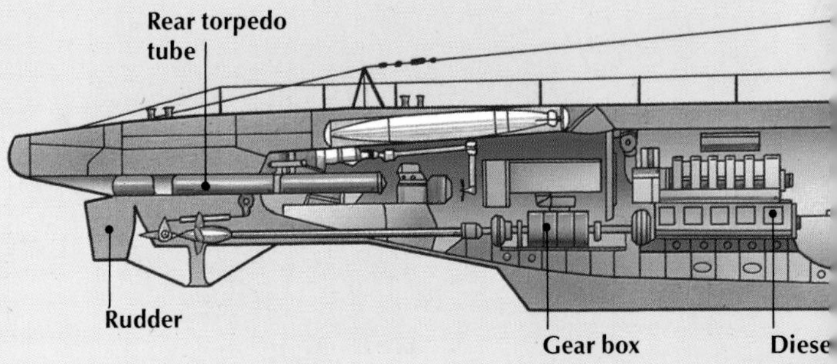

From 1941 onward U-boats hunted in "wolf packs." As many as 20 would attack a convoy to achieve maximum losses.

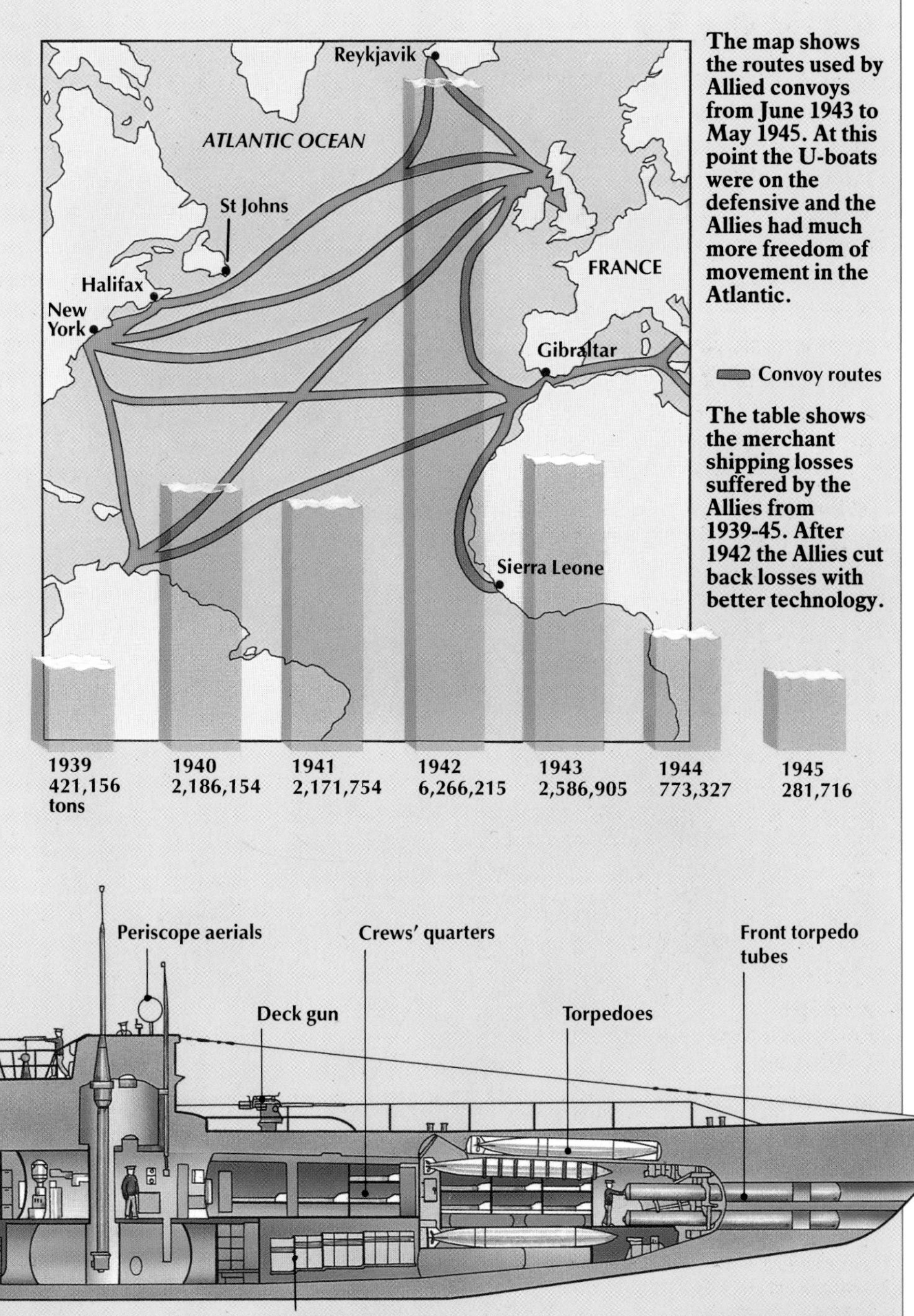

The map shows the routes used by Allied convoys from June 1943 to May 1945. At this point the U-boats were on the defensive and the Allies had much more freedom of movement in the Atlantic.

The table shows the merchant shipping losses suffered by the Allies from 1939-45. After 1942 the Allies cut back losses with better technology.

TRIUMPH IN THE WEST

The Allies had agreed on the tasks for 1944. While the Soviets would press the Germans back and away from the Soviet Union, the British and the Americans would keep up the pressure in Italy and prepare for a landing operation across the English Channel. In the East, Allied forces would concentrate on attacking Burma and closing in around Japan itself.

The V-sign for Victory was Churchill's trademark. He also urged on the British people with stirring speeches such as "Victory at all costs, Victory in spite of all the terror, Victory however long and hard the road may be."

The supreme commander of the invasion of France was the American Dwight Eisenhower and on June 6, 1944 130,000 Allied troops landed, establishing themselves despite stiff resistance from the German occupiers. Over the next two months two million troops joined this invasion of France. In Italy Rome fell on June 4 and the Allies continued to push the German armies back toward the Alps. At the same time huge Russian offensives brought the Red Army into Poland, the Baltic Republics, Romania and Germany itself. Soviet dealings with independent European nations, and Poland in particular, concerned Churchill. But at the Teheran meeting, in the interests of Allied unity, he had been unable to support the Polish resistance movement against Stalin's designs on their country. It distressed Churchill that Poland, for the sake of whose independence Britain had declared war

Allied troops disembark somewhere in Normandy, June 1944. The Anglo-American forces landed on five different beaches and faced stiff opposition on one of these.

against Hitler, might be passing under Soviet tyranny. But in the interests of the all-important alliance between Britain, the United States and the Soviet Union there was little he could do except protest and try to rouse the Americans.

Just as the Allies were poised to penetrate Germany itself, silent V1 rockets began to sow terror in London. Victory appeared to be in sight, but there was plenty of misery. The Allies broke out of Normandy in July and liberated Paris. In August, Allied troops landed in southern France and advanced on Lyons. Then in September the Allied advances in the Low Countries faltered when airborne troops failed to secure a bridge over the River Rhine at Arnhem. The Soviets took Budapest and General Leclerc captured Strasbourg.

Churchill celebrated his 70th birthday in November 1944 and among the many global issues facing him, Poland and Greece loomed large. After a meeting with Stalin in Moscow, he had reluctantly agreed to a Soviet-defined new border with Poland. In return he was given a free hand to back the anti-communist side in the civil war in Greece. In October 1944 British forces had intervened in Greece and for this undemocratic initiative Churchill was denounced at home, and risked assassination when he visited Athens. Meanwhile on the Western Front, the Germans made an unexpected counteroffensive through the Ardennes in December 1944. It was a desperate ten days before the Americans managed to drive them back.

Roosevelt kept the United States out of Churchill's "percentage agreement" with Stalin, also agreed in Moscow. This divided the Balkans

THE YALTA CONFERENCE

The Yalta conference was held from February 4-11, 1945. The Big Three decided that Germany should be divided into four zones of occupation after the war. The Allied leaders discussed the setting up of the United Nations.

However Churchill could not get Stalin to agree to hold free elections in Poland. Roosevelt would not support Churchill on this and it meant the Soviet-backed regime could crush any opposition. This led directly to the division of postwar Europe. Eastern European countries became Soviet satellites, allied to the Soviet Union in the Warsaw Pact. Western Europe became allied to the United States in the North Atlantic Treaty Organization (NATO).

The Big Three at the conference. Roosevelt was very ill during the conference.

The map shows the division of Europe into East and West following World War II.

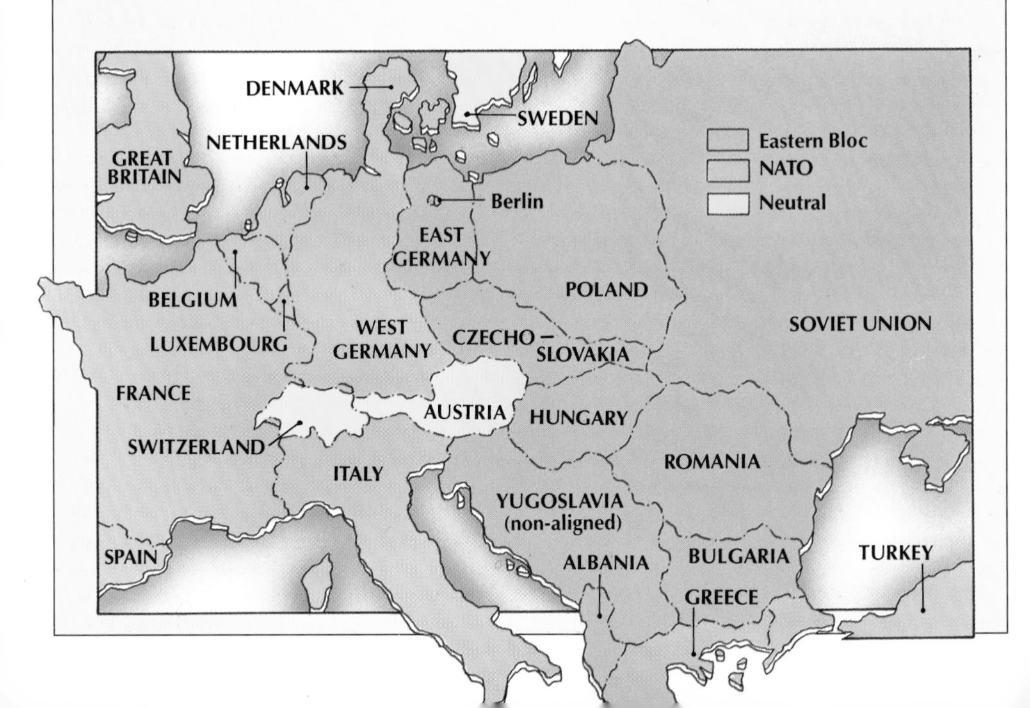

into zones of British and Soviet influence; for example, the Soviets would have 90 percent influence in Romania while the British had 90 percent in Greece. However, the United States did not stay out of discussions on Europe's future. Early in February 1945 the three leaders met at Yalta on the Black Sea to prepare for the end of the war and its aftermath. By then the Soviet armies were about 95 miles (152 km) from Berlin, nearer than that to Vienna, and in the north they had just taken Stettin.

Although the Yalta conference had been preceded by a Malta meeting between Roosevelt and Churchill, each of the two Western leaders expected to deal with Stalin on his own. Preoccupied with the structure of the future United Nations organization, and with the course of the war in the Far East, Roosevelt was less intensely concerned about Stalin's postwar designs in Europe than Churchill. Without telling the British prime minister, he made a secret deal with Stalin whereby the Soviets could occupy the southern Sakhalin and the Kurile Islands if Stalin declared war on Japan after the end of the war in Europe. Roosevelt then proposed the Declaration of Liberated Europe, by which all the European nations were to be free to choose their own postwar governments after free and democratic elections. This was a "gentleman's agreement," but in Churchill's view Stalin was no gentleman. He saw the Soviet army taking over vast sections of Eastern Europe and worried about where its advance would stop. From Stalin's point of view the superior economic power of the West, backed by the United States, was threatening the defensive system that he was trying to create, even at the price of many national freedoms.

In the rush for victory the Soviets now closed in for the battle of Berlin, backed up by an Allied bombing of all the major cities in the eastern part of Germany. The night of February 13-14, 1945 saw the RAF bombing of Dresden, an attack that was controversial because this particular city was packed with refugees fleeing from the East and it contained few targets of military significance. When the Western armies crossed the Rhine in March they raced through Germany, whose armies now lapsed into chaos. The American armies stopped on the Elbe because that was the demarcation line of the zone allocated to them at Yalta. Similarly, the British armies halted at Lübeck. The Soviets alone were allowed to liberate Berlin, Vienna, Brno and Prague. By April of that same year Roosevelt had died, and as well as

The city of Hanover in northern Germany lies in ruins following intensive bombing by the Allies during World War II. Churchill has sometimes been criticized for the decision to bomb the German cities. After the bombing of Dresden in 1945, Churchill made it clear he was not happy with the strategic bombing campaign.

THE DEFEAT OF GERMANY

The Allies divided Germany up into zones of occupation. So when the Allied armies reached Germany they stuck to their zones and stopped on the lines of demarcation. The British negotiated with Hitler's successor, Admiral Karl Dönitz. The surrender was signed at Rheims and Churchill and Truman declared that the war in Europe would end on May 8, 1945. Stalin delayed and the Soviets stopped fighting on May 9.

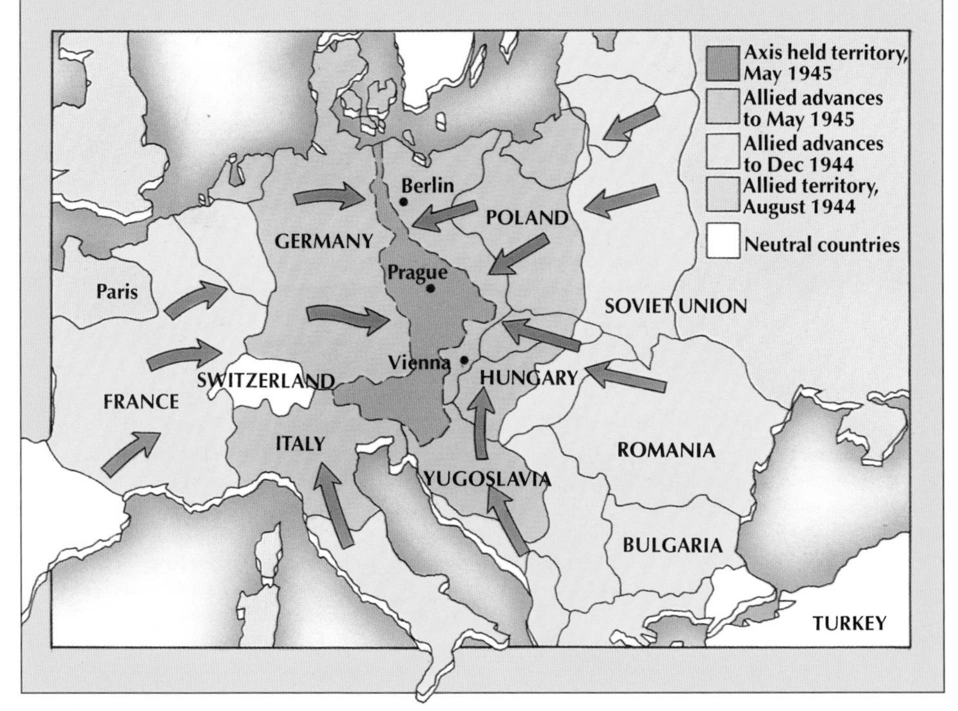

owing to a deep sense of personal loss, Churchill's international position was weakened by the American president's untimely death.

Long before Soviet troops had appeared in the suburbs of Berlin, Hitler had retired to an underground "bunker," seldom appearing above ground. On April 28, 1945 Mussolini was captured and shot by Italian partisans, members of the communist resistance, and his body was hung

British people celebrate Victory in Europe in May 1945. Churchill announced the victory to the House of Commons on May 8.

upside down over a market square. Two days later Hitler committed suicide. Later on that day the Soviets took control of Berlin. The unconditional surrender of all other German forces was signed at Rheims on May 7, 1945. (On August 6 a US bomber dropped the first atomic bomb on Hiroshima in Japan. On August 9 a second bomb on Nagasaki led to the Japanese surrender on August 15, 1945.)

At the VE or Victory in Europe celebrations on May 8, Churchill was the toast of Britain. In London, as he was being driven down the Mall to meet with the king at Buckingham Palace, a huge roar of acclaim went up from the enormous crowd which had gathered to salute him. Later that day his victory broadcast was heard over loudspeakers by the crowds gathered in the capital and throughout the rest of the country, and in many parts of the world, over the radio. But within ten days he had resigned as leader of the wartime coalition government. Parliament was dissolved so that a new government could be elected by the people. Churchill fought the election as the leader of the Conservative party.

While the votes cast in the general election were being counted – an operation that took time on account of the many soldiers voting overseas – Churchill went to the Potsdam conference, near Berlin. Once again he met with Stalin, and with the new American president, Harry Truman. The Soviet and the British leaders clashed over Poland: "My appeal came to nothing..." Churchill wrote.

Churchill with Stalin and the new American President Harry Truman (left center), at Potsdam in July 1945. It was the last Allied conference of the war and marked the beginning of the postwar "Cold War" between the superpowers, the United States and the Soviet Union.

The conference continued while Churchill returned to England to hear the election results. He had lost.

Although Churchill was widely admired and even revered as a national leader, the people on the home front, and the soldiers still at the other fronts, were more interested in the peacetime reconstruction offered by the Labor party's "Welfare State" than in a continuation of the superpower, global politics that were associated with Churchill. Also, it did not help Churchill that he was now identified with the Conservative party rather than the nation as a whole. Although the war years had brought many hardships to ordinary people, the emergency had produced some beneficial changes. To fight the war there had been rigid price controls and social

Churchill on the balcony of Buckingham Palace with King George VI and Queen Mary on VE Day, 1945. Later that day he addressed the nation "We may now allow ourselves a brief period of rejoicing; but let us not forget for a moment the toil and efforts that lie ahead."

services had been expanded. Measures such as subsidized milk and school meals, immunization against diphtheria and supplementary pensions had been introduced. People had learned to expect a fairer deal, and a land fit for heroes. In the hope of a future of peace, full employment and social equality the British electorate turned to the Labor party led by Clement Attlee.

It seemed a sad end to Churchill's political career, which was by no means over, but many people thought he had lost the election by his assaults on the "evils" of Labor party socialism. In an election broadcast he likened Labor party socialism to Nazism and even declared that "they (a Labor government) would have to fall back on

Churchill is swamped by crowds during the 1945 general election. After he lost the election he took on the role of elder statesman.

some form of a *Gestapo* (the German secret police)." The stirring language which had urged people on for the war effort lost him the post-war peace.

Conclusion

For six years, until 1951, Churchill was leader of the Conservative opposition in parliament. In 1946 he visited the United States, where he was fêted as a very grand old man with an important message for the world: "Above all, among the English-speaking peoples, there must be the union of hearts based on conviction and common ideals. That is what I offer. That is what I seek." What he sought until the day of his death was close Anglo-American cooperation in the face of a new division between East and West, a division represented, in his own words, by the "Iron Curtain." For thinking in such urgent, polarized terms so soon after the end of the war, he found himself, once again, denounced as an irresponsible warmonger. He was also interested in European unity, one way of reducing the possibility of further wars and of making sure that Britain would never be isolated again.

In 1951 the Conservatives were elected to office and Churchill was again prime minister. It was 51 years since he had first become a member of Parliament but now, although he continued to attend debates and vote, he could not speak with his old energy and passion. In 1953 the queen made him a Knight of the Garter. After this honor he became "Sir" Winston, but he later refused the offer of a dukedom because he did not wish to leave the House of Commons or to change his surname. In 1954 he was 80 years of age and a severe stroke forced him to curtail his public activities.

On April 5, 1955 Churchill decided to resign as prime minister. In retirement he worked on his *History of the English-speaking Peoples*, which he had begun in the 1930s. He also continued to enjoy painting, setting up his easel whenever he could. He died at home in January 1965 at the age of 91. After a lying-in-state at Westminster Hall, the funeral service was held at St Paul's Cathedral. The solemn funeral procession was watched by thousands of people in London and by millions more on television. Churchill himself had put some thought into how his funeral should proceed, its route, the hymns, and so on. In typical self-mockery, he called his funeral plan "Operation Hope Not." He was buried at Bladon churchyard, near Blenheim Palace where he was born.

Churchill's funeral procession took place in London on January 30, 1965. Millions mourned Britain's great wartime leader.

CHRONOLOGY

1874 Winston Churchill born at Blenheim Palace, Oxfordshire.

1888-93 Churchill attends Harrow School.

1894 Churchill's father, Lord Randolph Churchill dies.

1895-99 Churchill serves in the British army.

1899-1900 Goes to South Africa as a journalist to cover the Boer War; captured by the Boers, escapes and serves as a soldier.

1900-06 Churchill is elected as a Conservative member of Parliament.

1906 Becomes a Liberal member of Parliament (until 1922); serves as Under-Secretary of State for the Colonies.

1908 Churchill is President of the Board of Trade (until 1910); marries Clementine Hozier.

1910-11 Appointed Home Secretary.

1911-15 Churchill serves as First Lord of the Admiralty.

1914 World War I begins.

1916 Churchill serves in France as Lieutenant-Colonel commanding the Sixth Royal Scots Fusiliers.

1917-19 Appointed Minister of Munitions.

1918 World War I ends.

1919-21 Churchill is Secretary of State for War and Air.

1921-22 Churchill is Secretary of State for the Colonies.

1922-24 Churchill does not sit in parliament.

1924 Becomes a Conservative member of Parliament and also Chancellor of the Exchequer (until 1929).

1929-39 Churchill sits in parliament, but without office.

1939 World War II begins.

1939-40 Appointed First Lord of the Admiralty.

1940 May, Churchill becomes prime minister and Minister of Defense; June, France falls to Germany; July, Battle of Britain begins.

1941 Churchill negotiates Lend Lease Agreement with the United States; June, German armies invade the Soviet Union; August, Churchill and Roosevelt meet and draw up the Atlantic Charter; December, the Germans stop short of Moscow, the Japanese attack Pearl Harbor in Hawaii, the United States enters the war and Churchill and Roosevelt meet in Washington.

1942 January, 26 nations sign the United Nations Charter; by April, the Philippines, Malaysia, Singapore, Hong Kong and the Dutch East Indies fall to the Japanese; June, Japanese navy checked at the Battle of Midway and Churchill and Roosevelt meet in Washington; November, Montgomery wins the Battle of El Alamein against Rommel and US and British forces land in North Africa.

1943 January, Roosevelt and Churchill meet at Casablanca; the German Sixth Army surrenders at Stalingrad; May, Roosevelt and Churchill meet in Washington and Axis troops defeated in Tunisia; July, Allied invasion of Sicily; September, Allied landings in southern Italy; November, Teheran conference agrees to "unconditional surrender."

1944 June, D-Day landings in Normandy, France; July, the Soviets push the Germans back into Poland; September, Churchill and Roosevelt meet at Quebec and Allied troops reach the Netherlands; December, German counterattack in the Ardennes.

1945 February, Churchill, Roosevelt and Stalin meet at Yalta to discuss the future of Europe; April, Roosevelt dies and is succeeded by Truman; May, Germany is defeated by the Allies and Victory in Europe Day is celebrated; July, Potsdam conference with President Truman and Stalin, Conservative party loses the general election; Churchill becomes Leader of the Opposition (until 1951).

1951 Conservatives win the general election; Churchill becomes prime minister (until 1955).

1953 Churchill becomes a knight.

1965 Dies in London.

GLOSSARY

Allies the countries that fought against Germany, Italy and Japan during World War II – Great Britain, France, the United States, the Soviet Union and China.

appeasement the policy pursued by Neville Chamberlain of trying to satisfy Hitler by giving in to his demands.

Axis the alliance between Germany, Italy and later on Japan.

Battle of the Atlantic the crucial campaign of the war at sea. Fought throughout the war between German U-boats and Allied ships and aircraft.

Battle of Britain the battle waged over the coast and skies of Britain from July to September 1940.

Blitzkrieg lightning war – mobile armored warfare.

Bolshevik the name of the Communist party that seized power in Russia in 1917.

Chancellor of the Exchequer the British Finance Minister.

Congress the US parliament or law making body.

communism the belief that all property – including land and industry – should be owned by the community rather than by individuals. It is based on the ideas of Karl Marx.

democracy government by the people, through elected representatives.

fascism has come to mean anyone with extreme right wing views. It was used to describe the regimes of Mussolini and Hitler. Fascism was not a set of beliefs but more attitudes, for example, obedience to the leader.

Gestapo the German secret police.

Gold Standard the system which fixed the price of the British pound to the price of gold.

House of Commons the lower house of parliament in Britain.

Nazism stands for National Socialism, which was the term Hitler used for his party. It means an authoritarian, undemocratic regime.

radar comes from the US term Radio Direction and Ranging. It was a British invention. Radar is a defensive system which could detect aircraft by using radio waves.

parliament a law-making body. In Britain it is made up of the House of Lords and the House of Commons. The House of Commons has elected representatives known as M.P.s.

socialism the belief that income and wealth need to be fairly distributed, so some industry is owned by the state and taxes redistribute money from the rich to the poor.

Soviet originally meant a workers' council in Russia. Now it means part of the Soviet Union.

U-boats or ***Unterseebooten*** German submarines.

United Nations the organization set up after World War II to help settle international disputes without the need for war.

War Cabinet the leading members of the British government during a war, who take all the important decisions about running the war.

FURTHER READING

Calvocoressi, P and Wint, G *Total War: Causes and Courses of the Second War*, Pantheon Books, 1989

Churchill, Sir Winston *Great Destiny: Sixty Years of the Memorable Events in the Life of the Man of the Century Recounted in His Own Incomparable Words*, edited by F.W. Heath, Putman, 1965

Churchill, Winston *The Second World War*, Time Inc., 1959

Higgins, Trumbull *Winston Churchill and the Second Front, 1940-43*, Greenwood Press, 1974

Keller, Mollie *Winston Churchill* Franklin Watts, 1984

Messenger, Charles P. *The Second World War*, Franklin Watts, 1986

Natkiel, Richard *Atlas of World War II*, Military Press, 1986

Taylor, A J P *The Origins of the Second World War*, Antheneum, 1961

Taylor, A J P *English History 1914-1945*, Oxford University Press, 1965

INDEX

Photographic Credits:
Cover and pages 4, 7, 8, 10, 13, 17, 18, 21, 22, 26, 28, 29, 36, 37, 41, 44, 46, 50, 52, 53, 54, 55 and 57: Popperfoto; page 31: Robert Harding / Imperial War Museum; page 48: Topham Picture Library; page 42: Signal.

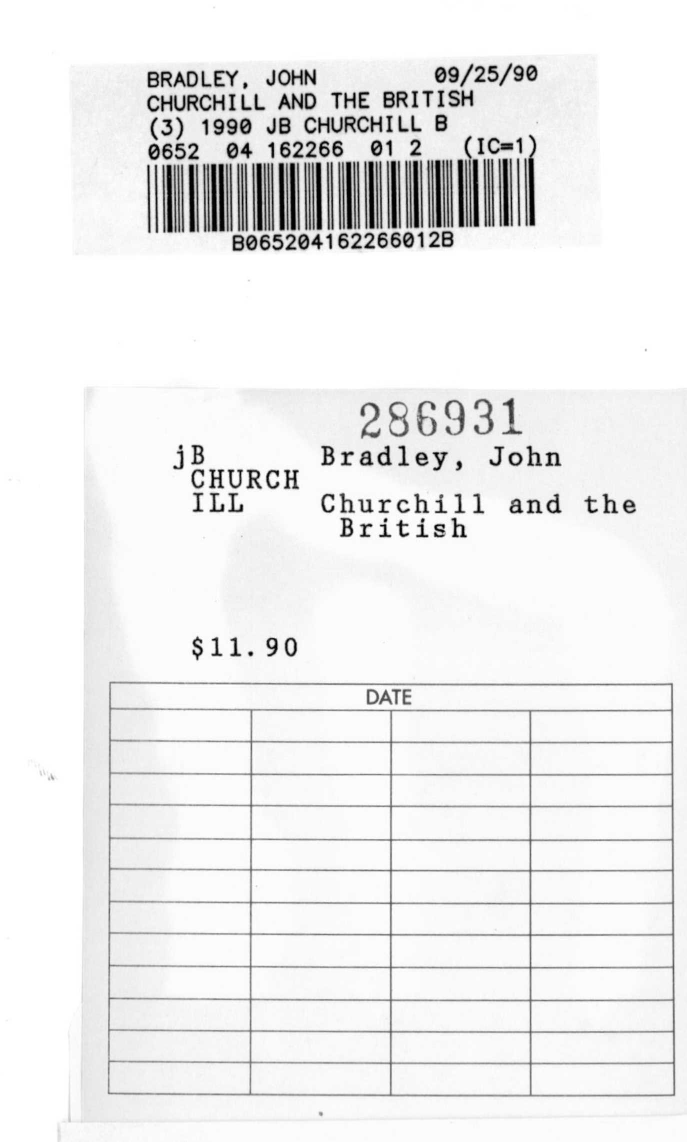